Broken Pieces

How the love for one man nearly destroyed my life!

By

Evangelist Linda Marshall Brownlee

Copyright © 1973, 1978, 1984, 2020 Evangelist Linda Marshall Brownlee

All rights reserved. No part of this publication may be reproduced, distributed, or transmitted in any form or by any means, including photocopying, recording, or other electronic or mechanical methods, without the prior written permission of the publisher, except in the case of brief quotations embodied in critical reviews and certain other noncommercial uses permitted by copyright law.

Scriptures taken from the Holy Bible, New International Version®, NIV®. Copyright © 1973, 1978, 1984, 2011 by Biblica, Inc.™ Used by permission of Zondervan. All rights reserved worldwide. www.zondervan.com The "NIV" and "New International Version" are trademarks registered in the United States Patent and Trademark Office by Biblica, Inc.®

ISBN-13: 978-1-951300-10-4

Liberation's Publishing LLC - West Point, Mississippi

Broken Pieces

How the love for one man nearly destroyed my life!

By

Evangelist Linda Marshall Brownlee

Table of Content

Acknowledgements 7

Introduction 11

Preface 13

The Loneliness 21

The Rejection 45

The Brokenness 55

Conclusion 67

My Prayer 69

Evangelist Linda Marshall Brownlee

Acknowledgements

Before I begin my story, I must recognize and thank God for inspiring me to write this book. He has allowed me to write this book. He has allowed me to taste the of the love he has for me and my life.

I want to thank Bishop Jimmy Jones and Co-Pastor Cora Jones of Christian Fellowship FGC. They have always been there to give me spiritual guidance when I needed it the most. I want to thank Pastor Annie Thomas of World Outreach Ministries and Bible Training Center, who prayed and helped me through many struggles.

My God sisters and prayer partners, who have been by my side throughout the toughest times in my life. Words cannot express my gratitude for all your love and support. You have prayed and comforted me along the way.

My children, who never left my side.

My children, who God blessed me with. They have prayed and cried with me, while assuring me everything will be alright. They were heartbroken just as much as I was, while still having strength to encourage me.

Christopher, Nancy, Robert Jr., and Victoria I want you to know I love you. I thank God every day for the gift of you. He has blessed me with each one of you.

I must thank God for my own mother who gave me life, Gladys Marshall. We don't talk much about my problems. She has never given me her take on the situations in my life. She would only say that it would get better one day. Mom has a very compassionate spirit. As I remember her, I see where I get my strength from. I love you for having a kind and loving heart. May God continue to bless you for all the love you give to me and so many others.

My father, the late Rufus Marshall loved me very much. He wanted only the best for my life. My dad and I had a very close relationship. We laughed together and cried. We were best friends. I love and miss him very much; I know that he is in heaven smiling down on me.

Evangelist Linda Marshall Brownlee

Introduction

As we go through this life on earth, we are faced with many challenges of hardships, difficulties, and even persecution. There are many other struggles and battles, which we often go through; that are more intense, even more painful, and severe.

These battles are often faced on the inside; they are the ones that take place in our hearts. Most of the time no one seems to know or care to know. We can't share them with just anyone, so we fight alone, lonely, desperate, and frightened. We wait endlessly for God to intervene on our behalf. That answer seems to be so far away.

Most times we already know that the outcome of most battles will be determined on how we handle the situation. **I have been broken for a purpose!**

This book tells the story of my inward struggles. As you read it, I pray the Lord encourages you. I pray that you come away from this trusting Him as He leads you through your "valley of the shadow of death." You will be victorious!

Preface

"God, why did you allow me to go through so many painful experiences? Was it so I could learn spiritual truths? Did I take so much difficulty, and so much hurt to understand you and your will? Was there an easier way?

As I sit in my room thinking about all the years that have passed, I feel grateful. I have learned so much. I still ask the question why God chose such a hard way for me. Only He could give me an answer. He created me and loves me more than anyone else does.

I was feeling lonely one day and God spoke in my spirit. He explained His reason to me. Things that we go through in life, though it seems bad, it does not mean it is working for our bad. After the experience is over, you will see this. You'll see how it works for your good.

I was on an assignment in my marriage.

No one else could endure this except me. My situation was designed for me to be victorious while many other would have given up. My life experience was to allow other people to see the goodness of God working through me and for me.

My family and friends thought I would lose my mind, because the love I had for my husband was unhealthy. I loved him too much and the devil used that love to try and take me out of here. He wanted to destroy me. When the devil knows God has great plans lined up for you, he will use anything to stop those plans, even those closest to your heart.

Sometimes you don't understand why it's happening. You'll feel like life itself has thrown you a curve ball and it hit you. This is how my journey begins. This is how the pieces of my life began to shatter. This is why the Lord spoke into my spirit the title for this book, Broken Pieces.

To help you understand imagine a

jigsaw puzzle. If you remember having one as a child, you will notice that there were many pieces of the puzzle. Being a child, you didn't really know where the pieces fit together. You start to grab the pieces and try fitting them together. The difference between being a child with a puzzle and an adult is as an adult you have the instructions to read.

Many of us never take the time to read, we just start putting the pieces together. Not seeing that they did not fit perfectly. This was my life. I thought the pieces were matched perfectly, but they weren't. I was fighting a battle that would end in destruction.

God's timing is always perfect, and there has never been a greater need than now for my story. I pray that this book will help you as much as writing it helped me. God's amazing love brought me through. God wants our lives to be changed and our broken pieces to be put back together. Like never before we need a word from the Lord to work on us, through us, and for us.

This is where I am right now, allowing God to use me for his glory. For all the heartaches that I endured; tears shed; lonely nights wanting to be held; all the rejection that left me so depressed I wanted to die; God had a plan.

No one really knows what goes on in another person's mind. We always assume that things are all good based off of the outer appearance. No one truly knows the heart of a man, but God. He knows the good and the bad of every man's heart.

When Jesus saved us, He gave us his joy, peace, assurance of salvation and eternal life. In our minds, we expect God to remove all the hardships and difficulties of our life from now on. We as Christians can enjoy an easier and more comfortable life than the rest of the world. Jesus did not promise us a worry-free life. He did promise that he would be with us always.

Jesus told us in advance that we would

suffer trials in persecution just as he did if we are to become his disciples on this Christian journey. As I travel this Christian journey, I have had my share of ups and downs. I never gave up. As I endured the pain and heartache the more difficult the experience the more, I appreciated God for keeping me. I realized as I was going through, he was still right there all the time.

Now I know how much compassion God has for me, when His son Jesus died on the cross. Being broken has truly allowed me to understand and remember the truth of God's word. It has changed my life. I look back upon my painful times, disappointments, and persecutions as opportunities for the Holy Spirit to build me up and mold my life.

Romans 8:20-30 reads, "For those he for knew he also predestined to be conformed to the likeness of his son, that he might be the first born among many brothers. and those he predestined, he also called, he also justified, he also glorified." (NIV) I know that all things work for those who are called according to God's purpose. Even though I know the will of God for my life, it still saddens my heart that two people who once loved each other couldn't make it last.

The worst part of it all was we both knew God, his word, and what He expected of us. People once looked up to us as being a man and woman of God; it hurt to disappoint them. They couldn't understand how two people who profess to love and served God, could not allow God to fix the problem. It is disturbing for this to happen. You cannot not make someone love you if thy do not.

As you continue to read this book, I am not judging or pointing fingers at anyone. This book is of my life and my life experiences. It tells how God took an ugly situation and work it our for my good. I want to encourage you. The same God who brought me through will do the same for you. It doesn't matter the situation. There is nothing too big for God to handle, always remember that while you are in the midst of your storm.

In the judgement we will stand before God and Him alone. This book will help you understand, while showing you how to overcome. It may seem hard while going through, but it's not. The sooner you realize God is there with you, it becomes easier. Turn it over to God, not man. People never know how to handle your situations. You must let it go and give it to God.

Let's begin the journey through my life!

Evangelist Linda Marshall Brownlee

The Loneliness

As I sit here thinking about being lonely, I remember the pain it causes inside. It's one of the worst emotional feelings you can experience. God doesn't want us lonely. This is why he created Adam and Even in Genesis. He creates man for woman and woman for man. God caused Adam to fall into a deep sleep, took of the rib of his side and fashioned a woman just for him. Genesis 2:21-22.

God gave Adam a woman, not two, three, or four. Just one. She would be his helpmate. They were no longer two, but one. Being one who shared everything. There was never a day in which those two were lonely. They shared each other's thoughts. They worked in the garden together. It is a good feeling to know, that when two people are together that they have each other's back. When sin creeps in so does trouble. If you don't turn it over to God, it will consume you.

I often ask God, "why?" Why does my marriage have to be so different? Why aren't we able to work together? Did God design it to fail? The questions could go on and on. Only God can answer them for us.

When the circle of love is broken loneliness creeps in. It takes over you physically, your heart aches and the pain seems to last forever. When this type of pain begins it makes you feel like the world is over and you have no life. Even though you are a Christian and you love the Lord, that doesn't take the pain away in your physical body.

The Holy Spirit comforts you when you need it most, but the ache is still there, and you feel no relief. It doesn't matter what you try. God was with me, but it still hurt. A broken heart is a broken heart. It's like a knife to your chest that won't stop jabbing you.

Living in a house that should have been my home with no love was devastating. No talking to each other, always arguing. I am wanting him to show me some type of affection. I wanted him to show he cared for me, and when I didn't get it, it only pushed the knife little deeper. Can you imagine a knife going in your heart just slicing and stabbing away? This is exactly how I felt. No relief.

This is how I was just wanting him to hold and touch me. I wanted him to assure me that everything was going to be okay. I didn't get any of that. He would just look at me like I was mold that he wanted to pluck away. I wondered how we got to this point. The things we once shared and all the love we had for each other was gone. How could that happen?

I wondered if he ever loves me at all. I loved him so hard, and I thought it was how I was supposed to love. I was submissive and obeyed him no matter what. I thought every man wanted a wife he could count on. I wanted him to have the very best. He was the king of our castle, the head of our house.

He was the man I once was proud to call husband.

I was the woman who wanted him to have it all even if I went without. My reasoning was, "if I gave him my all I would want for nothing. He would have my back." Little did I know, I was just a silly woman in love with what we used to be.

If you ever find yourself placed in this position it is really important to seek help. Putting anything or anyone on that high of a pedestal is a recipe for disaster. Giving anyone too much praise will be the both of your downfall. The bible tells us not to give that much praise to any person or object. If and when you do, it becomes your idol. This man was my all in all, and I was setting myself up for disaster.

Relationships shouldn't be one sided. No single person should have all power in a relationship. That's too much authority. Decisions should be made together. When not, it becomes an abuse of authority. I would walk through the house like a person without any life in them. I was just going through the motions. I tried to share how I felt and how much I wanted things to work out. I just knew in my mind that once the stumbling block had passed everything would be alright.

As days went by the situation became worst. I can't remember what I did from day to day. It was a blur. I didn't want to live at all. My reasoning was if I couldn't be with the one, I loved I didn't want anyone or anything. I had stopped eating and didn't know it. I would just sit in the room all day long just reading out loud to God begging him to fix the problem. I just wanted him to save our marriage.

All I know is I didn't want to live at all, that is what the devil wanted me to do. I focused on my problem so much that I couldn't think straight. The devil's intention was to cloud my mind. God was about to do something great in my life, and this was a big distraction. The love which I had for this man was unnatural. It was not what God wanted. The devil is good at getting you off of track. I knew the assignment God had for my life, but sometimes we try to hold on to everything that is in our path. We try to take it with us. God's word says we have to forsake all for the kingdom of God. All includes mother, father, sister, brother, or anyone one else.

At the time I didn't think of myself or what God wanted me to do; I couldn't even think of our children it was only him. It was just that the man I had given my heart to. I only focused only trying to hold us together, even if it killed me. I already felt dead not having him by my side the way he once was. I had made a vow to him and an oath before God.

No matter what I tried to do to cover up the pain it wasn't enough. I was going to extremes, adding extra things on to look more beautiful. It still wasn't enough. I would put my make-up on and try to look my very best; but I still could not cover up my hurt and pain. In my mind everyone could see how I felt. If I could then so could others.

I did not know whether I was coming or going. I was cooking, cleaning, and doing chores keeping the rhythm. I went to church and acted normal. I praised God. All while I was only a shell of a person. I was deprived of love in need of help. When our children looked at us, they would ask if I was okay. I could see the pain in their eyes.

That was on of the hardest things. Seeing the pain in their eyes. It saddens my heart to see my children react to my pain. They often told me they heard me crying at night. They tried to get me to do things, but I just didn't have the strength. They knew I loved their dad with every fiber of their being.

Nothing was ever good enough for that man. If I tried to get his attention, he always had an excuse. I never stopped trying. I was beginning to sound like a broken record. I questioned God on why my husband gave all of his attention to others. I wanted to know why we only pretended to be happy in front of others. Why couldn't he bring that charade into our real life. Whenever we went anywhere, they only saw the perfect couple. We always looked so happy together. We were such a beautiful couple. Why? Why? Why?

When we were alone, he acted as if he couldn't stand the sight of me. I was covering and faking so much for the world that it started to make me even sicker. All of this pretending was working on my body physically, and I didn't even know it. I was to the point of sleeplessness. I wasn't eating and my nerves were shot. My body ached all the time.

I started to use pain pills and energy drinks to take me through the day. It wasn't a good idea at all. The pills took away the pain and the energy drinks boosted me up. I became numb. I never told anyone about the pills before writing this book. I couldn't believe it myself looking back. I was so depressed. It got so bad that I ended up in the hospital with a life-threatening heart attack. Now that was bad!

This didn't even get his attention. He came to the hospital hours after my heart attack. The expression on his face was unbelievable. I could tell he didn't want to be there. I was a walking time bomb that had exploded. Love denied is a horrible thing. I love this man more than any person should love another person. I had given my heart to him for so many years.

Many people would have found something else to occupy their time. I didn't. I was alone and felt like no one cared about me at all. This wasn't true, but it's how I felt. I had six lady friends who prayed with me often. The prayed with me and over me. They could see that what I was experiencing was getting the best of me. They knew if I didn't get it together soon, I would have a nervous breakdown.

I was talking to God, but it didn't seem to be helping. I had put that man above God. I am sure God was not happy with me. You should never love someone to the point of not loving yourself. There was a constant battle going on in my mind at all times. God was speaking to me, but the devil was constantly lying to me. The devil wanted me to believe I was the one at fault.

When you give that much power to a person you lose the ability to think for yourself. This is where I was. As I think back, I know I didn't make it through myself. God was with me. If he hadn't been the devil would have drawn me so far out, I would have drowned. People to this day still remind me of how deeply I allowed that man to wound me.

I knew how to cover up the pain in front of others. Behind closed doors it was awful. It was my job to make us look good to others. In public we laughed with each other and joked. All while underneath I was a wreck. I knew that once we were out of the people's view my world would crash down again. We were back to normal not talking, touching, or anything else.

I wanted to reach out and just tell them that we were not the perfect couple. We were a complete mess. I couldn't tell anyone what was going on in our house. It was bad for our image. I wanted and needed help but was too ashamed to ask for it. In hindsight I didn't know how to ask for help. How do you tell people you've been putting up a false image? I suggested marriage counseling, but that was out of the question.

I did seek counseling for myself. My counselor told me everything I needed to do for myself. It was the same thing God had already told me. I was just not willing to let go. The children asked why we didn't leave. They wanted us to get help, while being concerning that they would be split apart from their parents. They hated the idea of us separating.

They kid asked other kinds of questions

too. I never had the answers. I wanted to, but I would have only told them a lie. Our children loved us both. They wanted to see us happy. They weren't being shown love. They suffered just as bad as I was, maybe even worse. I just kept quiet and went on living with things they way they were. To the world I kept pretending life couldn't be any better. I thought maybe that would give the children some peace. Maybe they would stop worrying so much.

Instead, things got much worse. One day I was driving home from school. God spoke to me. He said, "It's time." Immediately I knew what He meant. I cried, "No!" Tears began to run down my face. I knew what God was saying, but I ignored him and continued to drive. I tried reasoning with God. I said, "let me just keep praying for it to be alright."

God was telling me it was time to leave the house that was supposed to be my home. I was to leave the man I loved. I didn't want to hear this. I tried blocking it out. I had no idea that the worst was to come.

A few days past, and we hadn't argued in about a week. In my mind things must be getting better. I thought back to the day when God told me it was time to leave. I thought if I had left it would have been a mistake. Things are better now. Little did I know I was about to be in for a rude awaking.

Before the trouble started, I reasoned with God again. I said we're not arguing and fussing. I told God everything is going to be fine. Can you image me telling God anything? It was like I knew better than God. Because I disobeyed God all hell broke loose. It didn't take long either. The arguing came back with a fierceness. We fussed and fought all the time. I would try reasoning with him. I told him how much I loved and needed him. It was like talking to a brick wall. He wasn't moved.

After the fighting started back, I thought to myself why I lied all the time about our relationship to others. Why was I always trying to make people think we were happy? My husband never asked me to lie. He never asked me to say a certain thing to people. I took on the burden of trying to make us appear as something we weren't. Big mistake. I should have allowed people to see us for who we really were.

Who do I blame? Well the answer was clear, me. The only thing I did was place myself in a very unpredictable situation. I made myself look stupid. Let me explain my reasoning. As time went by, I was just a shell in his presence. My life had stopped, and everything was focused on him. I was concerned about where he was, what was he doing wrong, how I could get him to change. The list could go on and on.

His life continued as normal because all I did was focus on him.

Wrong! Wrong! Wrong!

It was not my job to fix anything. I was trying too hard. If things were going to get better, it had to be both of us working together. I can only give account of what I was doing. I could encourage him and ask him, but ultimately the choice was up to him to want to stay in this marriage. I stopped trying, but I still held up the lie when we were in public.

When people in the family and at church looked at me and asked what the matter was, I lied. I would just say I was tired. Knowing all the time that I was living a lie. Everyone that came in contact with us knew that something was going on; they just couldn't put their finger on it. Eventually is was just out. It couldn't be hidden anymore.

I knew who God was, and I knew that God didn't want me living like this. I didn't know what to do and I didn't want to let him go. I spent most of my time reading and praying trying to figure out how I was going to fix this mess of a marriage. I didn't want to lose my husband. I didn't want my family broken up. I never wanted my family to suffer from a split. All this had my mind spinning out of control trying to fix what was broken.

I thought that it was a wife's and mother's duty to fix everything in the house. We made sure the children were fed and clothed. I made sure my husband didn't lack anything. This is why it was so hard to please him in every way. It was my responsibility!

Every time I would think about what was going on with me and my family, I would get sick. I didn't want to really accept what was really happening. I was getting ready to take charge of my situation. I made up my mind that I was going to search for a house; maybe this would get his attention.

I looked for about two weeks knowing I didn't have any money to go anywhere. I was trusting God to work on my behalf. Maybe this would shake my husband up a little bit. This is what I hoped. I looked at several houses that day. I couldn't afford any of them. It dawned on me that I didn't have any money of my own, and my job was slow.

I knew I still had to leave, I just didn't know how or when. I knew it would be soon. I even told my husband what I was doing. It didn't faze him at all. Little did I know he wanted me gone anyway. Because of his lack of response, I sunk deeper into depression. It became too much on my physical body as well as my mind. My heart ache so bad all the time. It felt like it would burst out of my chest. I was at the point of wanting to die and not live on. My reasoning was I was dying anyway.

What kept me going was thinking about my children? I thought every day, "Lord, what am I going to do?" After that, my thought was if I was going to die, let me die trying. My physical body was really going through major changes. My hair started to fall out every time I combed it. I was losing more weight on top of the thirty pounds I had already lost. There was nothing I could do to stop it. I could get out of this situation before it killed me.

I found myself getting dizzy, wanting to pass out. Just the thought of me leaving my marriage sent me into a panic. Even so, I knew I had to be the one to leave. It was the house I had called home, but I still had to leave. I was tired of arguing all the time. I made up my mind, if he loved me, he would come and get me after I left. Now this was a chance I was taking. He might not come at all. But I decided to take a big chance.

Once you cross that line, you may not be able to come back. This is where I was, I was about to cross the line of no return. I looked and looked for a new home. Everything was so expensive. I wasn't making enough money. I started to cry as I thought about how I was a grown woman with no way out of a bad situation. I had to stay home a little longer.

I anointed everything in the house. I was behaving like Joshua in the bible. I started walking around the house seven time every night praying and anointing everything. The children knew what I was doing, and they didn't interfere. I knew that the enemy was trying its best to destroy me. This is what the whole situation was grounded on. It was the devil himself trying to kill, steal, and destroy.

The devil knew if he started stirring trouble-up in my marriage that I would break and bend to hold it together. That is exactly what I did. I was taking a beating trying to hold this marriage together.

It was a Sunday morning. I just couldn't take it anymore, I told him I was not going to church and these words came out of my mouth. I said I couldn't hear him anymore. Our life was just a lie and I was tired of pretending. God wasn't getting any glory out of this. It was time for this marriage to end.

I didn't go to church. I just went on doing things at the house as usual. I didn't have a car, so I was just there with the children. He went to church by himself. A lady who attended the church up the street had stopped by a few weeks earlier. She saw me standing in the yard. When she came to me, she said God had sent her to me for a reason.

She asked if I would like to go to church with her. I told her I would. I didn't have a car, but I wanted to go to church. I went with her every Sunday after that. I prayed and I laid at the alter for God to help me.

The next week, on that Sunday morning around seven a lady called me about one of the houses I had looked at. I was in the kitchen preparing breakfast when the call came through. She said to me that God had woken her up around three in the morning today. She said, she had to give me that house. She said she wanted to call me right then at three, but she knew it was too early.

I didn't have any money and my job was very slow. I told her my situation and she said don't worry about it. Just come by whenever you get ready and get the keys. Things were still heated up at home, and I just couldn't take much more. I was dying there and needed this way out. I did allow another week to pass. I thought about it, I still had a house waiting on me. I just hadn't picked up the keys.

That night I started to question God again, just to make sure I was doing the right thing by leaving. I didn't want to go, but this relationship was not healthy for anyone involved. Another week passed and I asked myself, "Why should I keep doing things like I'm happy. If God was not in it, it was not pursuing." I stopped pretending and our lives became separate.

I knew our personal life had nothing to do with the church. I was concerned about how the people would react. We were a couple who pretending to be happy all the time and so in love. The members believed this lie. It had gotten to the point where I couldn't do it anymore. My heart ached and the knife that was sticking in my back was going deeper and deeper.

As a woman loneliness was not good but being alone while you have someone is worse. You thought you would be with that person forever, eternity. Then you find out it won't even last until the children grew up. Feeling this way makes you loose faith in who you are individually. The devil will put anything in your mind to make you feel like it's your fault.

As I prayed that night I cried to God and said enough is enough. I can't keep going through the day to day and year after year fiasco or continue to lose myself in this relationship. I had to get my life back on track.

The next week I cried and prayed, because I was getting ready to make that major move. I gave it my best shot. I got up early and got my children together. I was determined to move forward. I was going to let God have his way. This is how it happened. My husband was headed out of the door, and I said wait we're going with you. He replied no he was going by himself. I told him these exact words, "If you leave without us, we won't be here when you get back." His response was, "fine." Then he went on to say, "do one thing for me don't tell anyone I put you out."

I smiled and said I wouldn't dare say that, I would say, "enough is just enough." So, as you can see everything seemed to have happened on a Sunday. I'm still trying to figure that out myself. I moved into my place and that would become our home.

I didn't have any money or a car. Before the day was over family and friends had blessed me so it was unreal. God had people there all the time just waiting for me to trust Him and make that move. If I am going to live in a house with a man that doesn't love me, I may as well be on my own. I should be letting God do what he does to work for both of us.

It's better to depart than to end up being

bitter to each other which was already starting to set in. Turning the situation over to God doesn't mean that I gave up on us. It means I will let God take control of this and whatever is the outcome I accept it. Let go and let God have His way, which is the only way I survived this storm. It wasn't easy, but I put it in God's Hands!

The Rejection

Have you ever wanted something so bad and someone told you that you couldn't have it? Well this is how it was for me. I was trying to give and share my love with someone who rejected it. No matter what I did or what I said It was rejected. My whole world was turning upside down, and I couldn't figure out why. Lord why me?

I kept asking this question over and over again. I couldn't get an answer. What was it about me that he couldn't love me as much as I loved him? I tried to show him in many ways just how much he meant to me. It still didn't help. I asked God to help me, but I didn't get an answer.

How can you share love with someone who keeps rejecting you? To be honest you can't. If they don't want it; then you can't force it. You will only make yourself sick and tired of trying. In my heart, I believe that everyone wanted someone to love them to the point, where you tried to give them all that you had and then some.

I asked this question, to myself. Was I trying to hard? This man doesn't have a clue, to the extreme that I went through just to make him happy. When I wanted to do things for myself, I sacrificed my needs for this.

I went without just to make him happy and he didn't even know. Either that was love or in other words, I just made a complete fool of myself. Who wouldn't do what I did? This is easy, not too many.

Being in love will make some people do stupid stuff, which they will only realize later that they should have let go. But I wasn't a quitter. I was going to keep going at all cost and I did. By doing this, it only made me sick and I wasn't happy with myself or my life.

Have you ever gone to bed with someone and they act like you weren't even in the there with them? Turn their back on you and you could not even touch them, without an excuse about being tired all the time. What kind of mess is that? How can a man lay next to his wife night after night and not care about her needs or her feelings at all? I will tell you, the one who doesn't care about you. When a love has turned cold, its cold and no gas can heat the flames.

Love once dwelled in this marriage, but it is now long gone. I have never wanted to be where I am not wanted, and there is nothing to accomplish but heartache and pain. The only thing that kept rolling over in my mind was rejection, rejection and I didn't want to be reject.

That even sounds bad; it is just like a toy going down the assembly line. Look it has a flaw, reject it because it is not good. That's how I felt, like I had a defect and couldn't be used anymore. If the man that I was in love with, rejected me then who would want me?

Who wants a woman who has been broken to pieces and her life is scattered?

What a way to go! How can I minister to someone and tell them that God can fix their relationship and my own went to pieces? I am wondering how God can take this ugly situation and use it to help someone else. I kept asking myself, who would want to hear me, woman whose life was a total mess?

I didn't know at the time, but God was going to use this very difficult time in my life to encourage all the people who reads this book. The people, that he would allow me to minister too; so that I will be able to tell them that God is still God. My desire in my heart and spirt was always to minister and encourage people, who have been broken or hurt.

Now, I know the assignment and ministry, that God was directing me in. To God, I am not a reject, I am a conqueror, because of Him I can do all things, because God is still God. My desire in my heart and spirit was always to minister and encourage people, who have been broken or hurt.

Now, I know the assignment and ministry, that God was directing me in. To God, I am not a reject, I am a conqueror; because of Him I can do all things, because God is giving me the strength to press forward in the mist of the storm. (Phil. 4:13)

You know why, because I am a survivor and I did it by grace of God and the love that He has for me. If He did it for me, He can do if for you. GOD knows, how much a person may endure so much pain and heart ache. God knew how Linda was going to respond to this situation. God already knew how the outcome would end.

Not every woman can survivor her storm and walk away, as I did. Now, don't get me wrong, I didn't say that I did everything right; but I never stop talking to God. I had to learn some things the hard way. Because I didn't want to listen to what God was instructing me to do at the beginning. I was trying to do everything on my own. You must trust GOD; to bring you through.

Yes, it hurts to let it all go, but in the long run it will all work for your good. It's better to walk away; than to end up hating each other. Staying will only make you become bitter as you continue to stay in your situation.

I had so many people there to help, but most of all had God on my side the whole time. God had never forsaken me. I was just so caught up in my feeling and what I wanted and that was to make myself happy. Not knowing or understanding the plan God had for my life.

Yes! I know that I am a minister and we all make mistakes; but if you don't obey God's commandment you will only allow the devil a campground to destroy your life.

I really couldn't see how I made it from day to day. I do know now that it was by the grace of God. He was covering and protecting me. When God has his hands on you there is no devil in hell that can destroy or stop you. I was on assignment.

My assignment was to allow other people to see God's goodness working in my life. Oh Yes! It was God working this entire situation out. There was no way that I could take credit for anything. God said, "Stand still!" I didn't want to go through the pain and the suffering, but who am I to complain. When I think back to how Jesus endured so much pain for us. Who am I to complain?

Being rejected made me feel like no one would ever love me. I asked myself that question. Why would they? Thinking of Jesus again, they rejected him for standing and doing what was right. Just because you have been rejected and unloved by one doesn't mean you'll never be loved again.

Everyday that goes by I love God more and more. The things that He has already done in my life and the things he is about to do make me want to serve him all the more. All the hurt and pain was embedded so deep in my mind; but this is how the devil wanted me to feel. He wanted me to feel that no one would ever want me or love me again.

The enemy was making me feel unworthy. He wanted me to be ashamed or embarrassed to be around my family and friends. I didn't feel worthy enough to walk down the street. I was ashamed to go in the store because people in the stores knew me. They would look at me with pity. They didn't have pity on me, but they knew what I had been going through.

Many people knew both me and my husband. To me that was enough to make me not want to be in the public. I only went to work, church, home and to the store if I had to. I placed myself in a box and refused to come out. This is exactly what the devil wanted and that's what I did. I could have stayed there to be honest; it was a safe haven.

I finally realized that the world was not against me. It was the devil still trying to suck me under. I had to try and find my way back into the arms of God. God was there waiting for me to reach out to him. He seemed so far away. I knew that God wanted to make this situation better. I just didn't want to let go.

God came in and fixed my life and restored all the pieces. He made my life better than it was before. I only had to let go of the situation. Though we were not in the same house my heart still ached for him. Love doesn't die overnight, at least not for me.

I just kept holding on to what was and not even looking forward to what God was getting ready to do. I was just cutting down my own blessings. It wasn't anybody's fault, but my own. I was so afraid of even trying to come out of the rut I had dug myself in.

My prayer partner just knew if I didn't come around soon there would be some serious problems to come. It was in my voice. The loneliness and the rejection. I kept sticking my hands in the fire and stirring it up. I was holding on for just a glimpse of him wanting me. The fire was consuming me. I talked with no life in my body. I know that doesn't sound right, but words were only coming out, but they made no sense.

I was about as low as I thought I could go, but little did I know that I was beginning to sink deeper. I kept setting myself up for pain and hurt. I know I had to trust God to take me through this ugly storm. I almost completely broke down. When the rain pours there is thundering and lightening coming too. I was in for a storm. After leaving I thought my life would be immediately better. No, it wasn't it just got worse. Even though I left It was just the beginning of heartache.

The Brokenness

After I left my husband, I just knew that he would come after me. He would come and tell me that everything was going to be alright. Two days had past before I heard anything from him. It was not what I wanted to happen. My heart broke in half.

I cried for days and it got worse with each day. In my mind I was wondering, "did I do the right thing by leaving?" This question just kept going over and over in my mind. I constantly kept a headache. I knew it was because God didn't want me living like this. No one should have to!

I eventually moved into a trailer lot. I didn't like it there, but it was my new beginning. I had to find myself. God wanted me to take this time to get Linda back. It was just me and my children trying to make it alone. I would sit in my room and cry all of the time. I wondered how I was going to do it all by myself.

My work was getting slower and I just knew the children and I would be on the street. Little did I know that God had sent and angel our way. The angle came to help with the heavy load of all of the bills I had. Was I scared? Yes! I still trusted God though. There were times I didn't know where our meals would come from and I didn't want to ask anyone for help, but I did. I wasn't going to let my children suffer. A mother will do what she has to in order to take care of her family. I did just that.

I called on God so much to do this and to do that, and He came through. I would sit in my bedroom. It was my safe haven. It's where I spend most of my time. I would sit there looking out of the window praying that the love of my life would come and get me. I was out but my heart was only thinking of him.

Day s went by and he didn't show up. Those days turned into weeks and he still didn't show up. I took it upon myself to finally go see him. I want to try and talk things out. Nothing good came from that either. I thought that If I put some space between us, he would see how much he missed me. It didn't. I was out and that meant no coming back. I had no idea that my plan would backfire. I took the chance to keep my own sanity.

I asked God again, did I do the right thing. I just wanted everything to be alright. I wanted our family back together. I did exactly what the enemy wanted me to do. I kept interfering with the plan of God. The enemy wanted me to keep interfering with the situation and try to make things work out on my own.

When you do this, it interferes with God doing his mighty work in the situation. Seriously if I could have done it myself our family would still be together, and I wouldn't be in this situation. Now us on my own it wasn't as easy as I thought it would be. I wasn't happy and my heart still ached for the man I loved. "God why can't you fix this mess?" Was the question I kept asking.

Being broken to the point of wanting my life to end. God was trying to get my attention, but I wasn't listening. God was trying to get me to focus on the real issue at hand and that was Him. I was so in love with a man. I put my wellbeing on the backburner. I was allowing the enemy camping ground to ruin my life and those who were closest to me.

Can a person love someone too hard? Yes, they can. You can love a person so hard until you no longer care about yourself or anyone around you. I loved this man so hard that I stopped loving me. The only thing I could think about from day to day was him. I would get up in the morning thinking of him. When I was at work people couldn't even talk to me, my mind was on him. When I went to bed at night my mind was on him.

I would cry all night thinking of him. Though I was seeking God, my focus was only on Him putting my marriage back together. So, I really didn't have a relationship with God anymore. I just wanted God to be God and put my marriage back together. It really is a serious problem when you begin to think only of your own feelings rather than what God has for you.

I was broken to the point of what I thought was beyond repair. My entire life as I had known it was going up in flames. I could do nothing about it or control it. I was so emotionally disrupted my needs no longer mattered. I tried to get a grip on my life, but I was too far gone at the time to do anything. I just waddled in my loss.

Can you imagine your life every getting to this point? I never thought I could, but this is where I was in a deep hole. The more I tried to see my way, the more I only thought of wanting to be with him. My mind was so clouded over all the hurt, pain, and loneliness. I didn't want to come back. I only wanted to die.

When I lay down at night I didn't care if I woke up the next day. That is how bad I felt. The mere thought of not having this man in my life was taking a tremendous toll on me. It was to the point I was willing to lose everything including my life.

I would drive sometimes from work and in my mind, I would think that maybe if I ran off of the road it would end it all. No one would even care. This is how bad I got. I wanted him or die. The devil wanted me to take my own life, because that was his intentions to destroy me. I know these are harsh thoughts, but love denied will make you do and think the most corrupt things.

This was the devil's way of really controlling my mind. I know what some of you must be thinking while you're reading this book. You probably are saying, "Wow! This woman must really be crazy. The devil wanted me to think I was crazy. When God has a plan for your life the enemy will try and do whatever he has to do to abort God's plan.

My prayer partner near and far started

praying and speaking blessing into and over my life. She prayed for God to touch my spirit. She encouraged me and help me to see that God had things for me to do. She prayed for me to become the woman that God called me to be.

Being the woman of God, this is who I always was. I had purpose, to serve Him to the best of my ability. Doing what God had called me to do nothing more and nothing less. The enemy wanted to stop me dead in my tracks by allowing the man that I loved to crush my heart.

God was trying to get me to release the man so that he could work on both of us. But little did I know I was trying to do what only God could do. As I think back, who was I trying to be? I can't help God; He was the only one that could fix or make us complete. Only when I take my hands off of the problem and only then could God do what he did best.

When you're in love most of us or at

least I thought I was. What was I doing? I wanted to put this ugly situation back in order. When I couldn't get it done, I tried to get help. Who was I kidding? People can't help you with your problems. Only God can.

God was trying to get me to let it go. I didn't want to let go. I thought I could handle it on my own. God was trying to get my attention, the very thing I was holding on to he wanted me to release. It was destroying me. If anything, or anyone is causing you to see things cloudy it needs to be removed.

I was trying to hold on to a relationship that I could never be happy in. I couldn't win because he didn't want me. It didn't matter how much love I had. I had to let it go. Even though I was praying to God, my flesh kept getting in the way. I was trying to fix a broken relationship. I was broken trying to fix a broke thing.

It took a good friend to tell me this; she said, "Linda everything that is broken is not intended for me to fix." I know now that everything that is broken is not for me to fix. It is better to let it go before it consumes you.

Not realizing I needed to repair myself my friend helps me to see clearly. She said, "look at yourself? What do you see?" when I took a long look in the mirror, I saw a broken woman. I looked broken to the point of no repair. As I looked into my own eyes I had so much pain more than I could have ever imagined.

The woman who I once was, she was gone. This woman in the mirror was so broken into many pieces. My very life at the time was just like a puzzle. Pieces of me were scattered everywhere. The sad part about it all was I was allowing everyone but God to try and piece it back together.

I thank God that I can now see the light. I finally allowed God to use me as he chose to. Being on this Christian journey is not always easy. If you continue to trust and hold on to God's unchanging hand you will make it. I will be able to overcome any and every obstacle in my life.

There is nothing too hard for God. We do have to trust him and do what is right. Trusting means letting go. God has so much more to offer us in this life. I can't see this with my natural eyes, but I know that whatever God has for me is for me. Man, women have tried to walk in my shoes and didn't succeed. My shoes were only made for me to walk in. My steps were ordered and ordained by God and God alone.

There are shoes that God has ordered for you to walk in; Walk in them. Let nothing stop you from walking into your destiny. God has a plan for each of our lives. If we would only trust him. God wants us to love Him and to have a love for Him in the form of worship. To give Him praise continuously. If we obey God and do his will, He will bless us with our needs and give us the desires of our heart.

We must read his word and follow his instructions. There is no other way. His words are a light when we find ourselves in a dark tunnel. There is no valley too low that God can't pull us out of it. I know firsthand. He pulled me back to the surface and he can and will do the same for you.

The love I had for one man nearly destroyed my life. For exactly one and a half years I took this time to seek God and find Linda. To be in his presences and to allow his spirit to flow within me. There is no greater feeling than to feel the spirit of God within you. It will give you unspeakable joy and assurance that you cannot find anywhere else.

I have devoted my life to God and to be used for his glory. When that time comes, God will bless me with my soulmate. The one who will love me, respect me, for the woman that God has called me to be. Who I am and who I represent?

Evangelist Linda Marshall Brownlee

Conclusion

Learning to let go of your past is one of the hardest things to do in life. Your past can and will destroy you as a person if you do not take control of the situation. It's like bouncing a ball. When that ball is in your hand you are in control, but when you let it go it's out of your control. Life is the same way in a sense; you have the power to take charge of every situation that happens in your life.

Rather your choices are good ones or bad ones it's your choice. You have to live with them. I have truly made some very difficult and wrong choices. At the time I made them they would have taken me out of this world. That is what the devil wanted. Philippians 4:13 states, "I can do all things through Christ Jesus who strengthens me." Not some things all things.

We as Christians must realize that there is power in the name of Jesus, which is stated in God's word. He didn't change.

That same power applies to us today as believers. We have the power not just to climb that mountain; but for the mountain to be removed!

My Prayer

Lord, please use my life that others may see your goodness working in me through me and for me. I was broken for a purpose. I was being molded and transformed by the Master's hands. I found strength in "God's Presence." While overcoming a season of being lonely, rejected, and broken.

God has allowed me to taste the true meaning of love. That is the love He has for me. I am my Holy Father's daughter and He wants the very best for me!

Evangelist Linda Marshall Brownlee

www.ingramcontent.com/pod-product-compliance
Lightning Source LLC
Chambersburg PA
CBHW030200100526
44592CB00009B/377